DAMAGED WOMEN AND HOW TO REHABILITATE

God loosed her and she glorified Him
Luke 13:10-13

LORNER J. JONES

Bloomington, IN  Milton Keynes, UK

authorHOUSE

AuthorHouse™
1663 Liberty Drive, Suite 200
Bloomington, IN 47403
www.authorhouse.com
Phone: 1-800-839-8640

AuthorHouse™ UK Ltd.
500 Avebury Boulevard
Central Milton Keynes, MK9 2BE
www.authorhouse.co.uk
Phone: 08001974150

This book is a work of non-fiction. Unless otherwise noted, the author and the publisher make no explicit guarantees as to the accuracy of the information contained in this book and in some cases, names of people and places have been altered to protect their privacy.

First published by AuthorHouse 12/16/05
Second publishing by AuthorHouse 5/11/2009

ISBN: 978-1-4208-8317-6 (sc)

Printed in the United States of America
Bloomington, Indiana

This book is printed on acid-free paper.

I would like to take a minute to talk about a woman who had an infirmity for a very long time. What do we call a long time? Well it can be hours, minutes, or only seconds. When you are going through turmoil it seems like forever, and that it will never come to an end. It's not the length of time that we are dealing with it's the miserable situation. I want you to know the greater the struggle the greater the victory. Know that your struggle is almost over, and help is on the way.

Luke 13:10-16; And he was teaching in one of the synagogues on the sabbath.

11 And behold, there was a woman which had a spirit of infirmity eighteen years, and was bowed together, and could in no wise lift up herself.

12 And when Jesus saw her, he called her to him, and said unto her, Woman, thou art loosed from thine infirmity.

13 And he laid his hands on her: and immediately she was made straight, and glorified God.

How many of you know that God will take your misery, and turn it into a Ministry? If I had to talk about verses ten through thirteen I would say; *God loosed her, and gave her an immediate healing.* The woman was bound along time but God gave her a speedy recovery.

14 And the ruler of the synagogue answered with indignation, because that Jesus had healed on the sabbath day, and said unto the people, There are six days in which men ought to work: in them therefore come and be healed, and not on the sabbath day.

15 The Lord then answered him, and said, Thou hypocrite, doth not each one of you on the sabbath loose his ox or his ass from the stall, and lead him away to watering?

16 And ought not this woman, be a daughter of Abraham, whom Satan hath bound, lo, these eighteen years, be loosed from this bond on the sabbath day?

If I had to preach verses fourteen through sixteen right now my subject would be *remember the Sabbath for your healing.*

That's just like folk they don't want to see you prosper. Everyone gathers in the sanctuary on the Sabbath to hear the word of God. Then there's an altar call after the word of God goes forward. Altar call is time for healing and deliverance, and that's a good thing to get healed on the Sabbath? If I'm sick or afflicted just heal me I'll be grateful no matter what day of the week it is. It really doesn't matter what day of the week Jesus heals, because He is in control, and He has all power in His hands. All Jesus has to do is speak it, and it shall be done. What should be our main focus is being healed, and remembering who healed us.

Many times we hear about someone who has been violated. Some tell, while others are afraid too tell, because they are emotionally fragile. Some think if they do tell that no one would believe them. Victims believe they've brought this on themselves and it's their fault. Many just don't say anything keeping the devastation of what happen to them to themselves. By doing so many times their lives are ruined because they don't have a healthy relationship. Some usually go insane; attempt suicide, or become drug addicts this will lead to the need for psychological therapy. Only to realize it didn't help, because the feelings are still present, and allow the victim to continue to live in fear. Many times when we are violated and the violator wants us to keep it a secret. You must remember it's not us who needs help it's them. You need to know that keeping this secret cause both of you pain. You are in pain because you want them to stop. They are in pain because they can't stop. It's really not them it's the demonic spirit that lives inside of them. Some people don't believe in demonic spirits. I want to let you know that they are real.

Mark 5:1-9, And they came over unto the other side of the sea, into the country of the Gad'-a-renes.

2 And when he was come out of the ship, immediately there met him out of the tombs a man with an unclean spirit,

3 Who had his dwelling among the tombs; and no man could bind him, no, not with chains:

4 Because that he had been often bound with fetters and chains, and the chains had been plucked asunder by him, and the fetters broken into pieces: neither could any man tame him.

5 And always, night and day, he was in the mountains, and in the tombs, crying and cutting himself with stones.

6 But when he saw Jesus afar off, he ran and worshipped him,

7 And cried with a loud voice, and said, What have I to do with thee, Jesus, thou Son of the most high God? I adjure thee by God, that thou torment me not.

8 For he said unto him, Come out of the man, thou unclean spirit.

9 And he asked him, What is thy name? And he answered, saying, my name is Legion: for we are many.

Many times people don't know how to be released from what has them bound. Most of them never seek help, and most of them don't do a lot of reading. We need to understand if we don't have faith; we don't have power.

Matthew 17:14-20, And when they were come to the multitude, there came to him a certain man, kneeling down to him, and saying,

15 Lord have mercy on my son: for he is a lunatic, and sore vexed; for oftimes he falleth into the fire, and oft into the water.

16 And I besought him to thy disciples, and they could not cure him.

17 Then Jesus answered and said, O faithless and perverse generation, how long shall I be with you? how long shall I suffer you? bring him hither to me.

18 And Jesus rebuked the devil; and he departed out of him: and the child was cured from that very hour.

19 The came the disciples to Jesus apart, and said, Why could not we cast him out?

20 And Jesus said unto them, Because of your unbelief: for verily I say unto you, If ye have faith as a grain of mustard seed, ye say unto this mountain, Remove hence to yonder place; and it shall remove; and nothing shall be impossible unto you.

Demons are real, and even thou the disciples walk with Jesus they had little faith. They could not cast the devil out of the child because of their unbelief, and lack of faith. Same way with us we don't think we are strong enough to break the chains that's holding us down. When you are going through turmoil you don't know what you are doing, because your mind is not right.

That's also hard for some people to believe, because they think you should know right from wrong.

The Bible tells us in *James 1:14-15; But every man is tempted, when he is drawn away of his own lust, and enticed.*

15 Then when lust hath conceive, it bringeth forth sin: and sin, when it is finished, bringeth forth death.

Whenever you are in the flesh you do things of the flesh. What we must remember we cannot control our own flesh.

Romans 7:18a For I know that in me (that is, in my flesh,) dwelleth no good thing.

Romans 8:5a states; For they that are after the flesh do mind the things of the flesh.

I have learned over the years that the only way you can get rid of various kinds of demons is to you summit yourself to God.

James 4:7 Submit yourselves therefore to God. Resist the devil, and he will flee from you.

Many times we don't know what's in someone's past, how he or she was raised, or what he or she endured as a child.

The question is were they violated as children or is this something that happened since adulthood? This is the reason why we as people need answers. We need to talk about this and not keep it hidden. Our children are being missed used in ways you can't image. We need to find out why some people became as violent as they are. Whenever you can kill, rape, molest, or brutalize someone and don't think twice something is definitely wrong. We will never get help if we keep our problems in darkness, and believe me, I know help is what we need for this type of situation.

It's not easy living in fear, because being afraid all the time is not natural. The reason children become a victim at an early age they can't defend themselves. Especially in a difficult situation like being attack by an adult, because children can't fight back. I will always ask this question why do we prey on the innocent? When you are a child you are already sacred, so you can't talk with authority because you are a child. Has this ever happen to you? Can you answer this question with honesty or are you afraid? As adults, when we are faced with an unexpected situation we tend to get speechless ourselves. It's not hard to believe that children are terrified, because we as adults are also. We keep secrets about things we need to tell because we are afraid. Children are not out spoken in that way. Most of the time children are afraid for their parents. Why? Their attackers threaten the parent in order to get away with what they are doing. Is the reason we have Pedophiles, because they have no authority or control at home? So they go where they know they can use authority, and that's on someone who can't fight back.

Parents should talk to their children, and explain at a young age the facts of life. Parents need to instill in their children that some people are not to be trusted, no matter how nice they seem. Here are some steps all parents should take with their children. Be sure to explain to your children not to get in the car with people you know, and especially people you don't know. Make sure to tell them to always call home whenever they are not sure about something. Teach your children to never give out personal information. Make sure you and your children have a secret pass word that only you and your children know. Parents should always know where their children are. Let them know you are there for them and they can tell you anything. Talk to your children and let them know how much you love them. Please make sure you discipline them they will thank you later. Your children need to know they can come to you for whatever they need. When you scream and yell at them you lose their trust in you, and it makes them bitter at you.

Sometimes we want to tell, but can we, will we, the question is do we have anyone we can trust to help get us out of this horrible situation? What sister, brother, mom, dad, or relative do you know you can we go to for help? Is help near us or is it far away, how long does this go on before I'm free, free from being taking advantage of, free from being violated? Can I get my identity back, or will I continue to be someone else? I'm a robot, because I'm doing what I'm told to do not what I want to do. Will I be rescued today or is today another day like yesterday or the day before or last week? Do I hate to see my family members coming? Why can't anyone realize what's going on? What's happening to me? Do I look like I'm all right? Do I look afraid? Am I not showing that I need help. If so, why is this still happening to me? Am I saying I need help out loud or am I just thinking it in my mind? Can anyone hear me? Maybe I'm not saying it loud enough. Hello, can anyone see or feel the pain I'm in? How do I get the words from my mind to my mouth so that I can ask for help? When I get this terror to my lips to speak it, whom can I trust to tell this nightmare with? How do I explain what is happening to me? What did I do to deserve it? I'm only a child. I was always told to listen and respect my elders because they are right, so what do I do to be free from this bondage? I have been branded and violated, its time for this nightmare to be over, when I wake up will this dream be over? Then I realize this is not a dream it is reality. Many times we don't know where to go and get help. This ordeal happens to a lot of children we know and don't know. It's time for us to find away to stop this violence. They try to deal with their problems by themselves, and it's not easy. Here are some of the things that take place when they can't deal with it. You have suicide attempts, low self esteem, no joy, not confident in any thing you do, always sad, bad relationships, walking around with your head down all the time, just all kinds of problems that you can't fix yourself. Most children go through bad situations when they are afraid to speak out. People we know and some we don't know are living with this fear everyday.

The reason I (Lorner) know is I also was in a similar situation. I know how it feels to be violated, and not being able to trust anyone. When I did tell I was called a liar, and no one believed me. That's when I decided when I would take matters in my own hands. I wanted to do my own revenge because I didn't know how to deal with the situation. There were terrible thoughts going through my head it was very hard to control. The hate was just boiling in my veins, and I wanted to see someone else hurt like I was hurting. All my life I swore "when I became an adult I would be strong enough to kill those who violated me." Often times "I wondered how could I harm them without anyone knowing what I have done." I "figured if they could get away with what they had done I could also." I often said "just wait until I become an adult, I will show them they wouldn't live any longer." I had hate in my heart for men, I thought about this all the time, stuff like this keep you from resting at night because you turn violent, or you withdraw yourself from everyone. There's a lot of unanswered question I needed to know. When I became an adult I wanted to know their location? What I really wanted to know, are they married, and living like they never done anything, and how many others have they hurt? Do they have children, and are they girls? What about a job, do they work? Is their mind free from sin or are they still stalking others? I thought about that all the time, what would they do next? I don't have to put names in this book, one thing about the truth it will find you no matter where you go.

My grandmother use to say you can fool some of the people some of the time, but you can't fool all the people all the time, and you can never fool God.

Ecclesiastes 12:14 For God shall bring every work into judgment, with every secret thing, whether it be good, or whether it be evil.

It doesn't matter if people don't know about the evil others do. They might hide it from some, but God knows all about it, and he will judge you. That's one reason I didn't carry out with getting even. I don't know why I was fooling but myself in thinking I could committee a crime. I couldn't do it knowing I had to live in a four by eight cell for the rest of my life. I needed to do something to satisfy myself? I wanted some relief, but at that time I didn't know how to get it. So many sleepless nights, always needing some closure, still couldn't trust. I didn't know how to trust because I had been so damage I didn't care about anyone. When we think of being damage we think of a woman in a domestic violence relationship only. It is more to it than we think, because you can be damage in many ways.

There's a lot of Damage Women, through out the entire Country, and every two minutes a woman is being rape. Only thirty percent of them report the rape, and only two percent is actually caught and convicted.

My opinion is I think there shouldn't be a stature of limitation on rape. A rape case should be treated as a murder cold case, because a part of the victim dies at the hand of her attacker. Many predators' stalks, rape, and then kill their victims. If the victim survives that's more terror she has to live with. If she identifies him she has to face him in court. After the trial is over his sentence is only three years that's not justice. If the predator is never located the victim is still scared of what might happen to them later if he's not caught. What amazes is when suspect is caught their bond is so low they can bond themselves out, and be on the prowl again. "I think whenever someone takes advantage of someone with a crime against nature, they shouldn't be allowed to bond out of jail." Especially when children are involved, and their bond needs to be in the millions. Rape is on the rise people, and it's time to get rid of this demonic fungus. In this book I the author (Lorner Jones) file a petition to have all rapist and predators remanded to a holding cell, and not be released. _____

Maybe if the victim knows their attacker is locked up they might tell. When you tell and talk about thing sometimes it eases the pain. For the victims that don't reveal their rape they will continue looking for someone or something to ease their pain. They don't know which way to turn or whom they can turn too. Everything is just one big mess, but many of them wants help but don't know how to ask for it.

Many are still afraid; this is a lot of weight to carry around on your shoulders. It's very hard for them to get on with their lives, still not trusting anyone, and when they do have enough courage to leave the house they are always looking over their shoulders. Most of them are always looking around, and get very nervous at the smallest sound.

What kind of life is this? It's time to get help. Many rape victims are very sacred to go out after dark. Some people say that's not that difficult, how can she still let that upset her? It's been so long ago when that happen to her. It's an easy thing for someone else to say if they have never been through something like rape. It's not something that is easily forgotten. It's own your mind everyday all day. If you don't deal with what happened to you it makes you lose total control of your life, and you remain angry at the world until you get help. That's why it's very important that you seek help early as you can. If you let this go on and on, it get harder and harder to deal with. Many people say girl God is not going to put no more on you than you can bear. The statement is not worded in the Bible exactly like that, but I guess it can also mean the same thing.

1 Corinthians 10:13 states; There hath no temp-tation taken but such as is common to man: but

God is faithful, who will not suffer to be tempted above that ye are able; but with the temptation also make a way to escape, that ye may be able to bear it.

But it's up to us to seek help from God in order to bear our heavy burdens. God said he has an away of escape for us and we need to take advantage of what he said and give it to him. If we give all unwanted burdens to him we wouldn't have to bear it. I feel like whenever you talk to people and tell them different things about what God say, you need to know where it is located in the Bible in order to get the right help that they need. If you never had anything weighing you down, you can speak out of term about someone else's life. Whenever we try to talk about someone else life we need to look at our own skeletons first.

Here are just some examples of some women that have been damaged. These are familiar stories that have happen to women all over the country. After you read these stories this could have been or might be you. These are not my stories, but I know someone can relate to them. I will talk about issues later.

There was a woman that had been married for twenty-five years to her high school sweetheart, and one-day he decides he no longer wants to be married.

She never worked before, because her husband wanted her stay home with the kids.

She had no experience in anything, but being a housewife. Suddenly her perfect world had come to an end. Fear set in then suicide thoughts came to her mind, so she began to question herself. What has change in our marriage? Why doesn't my husband love me anymore? What did I do? I don't know how I will make it, all the kids are grown I can't get child support, he left and told me I can have the house and the car, but the car has a payment book attached to it, what do I do? It happen just that fast, I cooked breakfast this morning, I went met him for lunch, at the supper table that night, he explain to me he no longer wants to be married to me, how do I move on with no work background? Somebody please tell me, after all I gave this man my whole life, then he destroy everything in one day, what we had built together all these years. Am I a Damage Woman? Yes I am.

That has to be really unbelievable you have given that man all those years. Then one day he decides that's not what he wants. I call that wasted days, wasted nights, and years.

Here is another situation; I know this happen in some places. My husband and I are very happy; we have three wonderful children. We are always there for all the PTA meetings, track and field, spelling contest, football games, and everything that good parents does with their children. My husband always treats me like I'm a Queen. I also treat him like a he's a King. I always brag on my husband, about how well he treats me, when everyone is talking, I just take over the conversation. I don't let anyone get a word in edge wise; it's all about my husband and me. I just go on and on with the conversation then someone asked the question, in a whisper. Can her marriage be that good? I replied to her I heard that and yes it is, then "I asked my question out loud are you jealous?" Then "I said to her keep your negative thoughts to yourself." Late one night I fell asleep, at least I thought I was asleep. "I kept wondering to myself could this be a dream?" But it had already happen the day before. I thought I was dreaming, when one day I had to go pick up Junior from his evening football practice.

I was running late, the only way to get to the school on time, I had to take the scenic route, meaning, (the back or side road). On the way there I say a truck that resemble mine at the gas station.

When I look in passing up the station, I saw a man and a woman walking into the store. They were holding hands, they briefly engaged in a kiss, but they didn't notice me passing by. When I seen this I couldn't believe it, so I called one of my friends. My hands were so nervous I could barely dial the phone number. With a voice of panic, I ask her could she go pick up my son from football practice. I quickly turn my car around, and waited until they got in the car. Then I followed them to see where they were going. I knew my husband was supposed to be at work. As I continue to follow them, they drove up to a motel. When they stepped out of the truck, they couldn't let each other go. Then I remembered that's the way we use to do. When we first met we were always together when you seen one you seen the other.

As they was walking to the room, he was holding her so tight, I couldn't recognize the woman at all, she had on sunglasses and a hat, so I let about three hours pass just sitting there. Then I finally said to myself, "I got to find out who this woman is." I went to the motel office, and explained to the desk clerk that my husband and I went down the street to the gas station, and locked the key in the room by mistake. I showed him my license, and who I was then he gave me the spare key. I tried to prepare myself for what I was about to see, but I knew it wasn't going to be good. So I took a deep breath, and tried to build up enough nerves to stick the key in the door. My hands began to shake out of control. I knew I had to do it so I finally stuck the key in the door. As I begin to open the door all I could see is my husband in bed with another woman. They were so involved with what they were doing; they didn't hear me enter the room. I just stood there with disbelief, and my heart was torn apart. While I was standing there inside of the room I cleared my throat to get their attention. They both looked around at me at the same time. Suddenly they became terrified, "I said to him this is not the man I know as my king." Especially with another woman, and as she turn more where I could see her. My husband was sleeping with one of my friends, then he said to me I can explain. "I said to him I can to" you are just like all the others. Out of all the times I was bragging on him she would always have a smart comment to say.

Now I know why she always had something negative to say. All that time she was having an affair with my husband isn't that a pretty picture. I guess is true what they say the wife or the husband is always the last one to know.

Am I a Damaged Woman? Yes I am.

Here is another situation, my husband and I live in a small town population six thousand or less, our children goes to a good school. But I'm the only one that is involved in their school activities. My husband stays to busy, and he is always working overtime. Even though he has a good paying job, he is always working a lot of overtime. I really don't understand why he works so much. He says it was to make sure we have everything we need. Its not often we do the family thing, because my husband is at work all the time. We use to do outings all the time it was lots of fun, but we don't anymore. I understand he wants us to have the best. I need some of his time too I think the kids will also agree. My husband gives us whatever we need, and all our wants. He's never said he couldn't give us what we wanted or y'all don't need that.

Our children love us very much, and they make it known to everyone they come in contact with. One day something strange happen, the school that my son attend was having a father and son day, and my son wanted his father to go with him. His father told him that he couldn't go because he had to work and he couldn't get off that night. Being broken hearted he were sitting with some of his classmates, and they notice he wasn't himself. They begin to question him, why was he looking like he had just lost his best friend? Then my son begins to explain to his friends. His father couldn't attend the father and son day, activity at school. His friend told him, his father couldn't go either, because he also had to work, and he couldn't take off. Then my son begin telling his friends, how he would like to see his father take off work, and come to just one of his activities at his school. His friend made the remark our dads must be important on their jobs, because everybody else dad is going to be there. Then my son said "oh well maybe next time he would be able to go". So his friend ask him where do your dad work, and he told him. He said my dad work there too. My son ask him what's his dads name, maybe my dad might know him. His friend told my son what his father's name was, and replied do you know him? My son with his heart pounding heavily, then he swallowed very hard and said no. My son asked his friend do you think we can get together later and do something? His friend with aloud and cheerful voice said oh yes, yes we can. Would you like to come over for supper later on this evening? My son asks his friend where did he live? He told him he lived on the north side of William's street. My son say oh that's funny because I lives on the south side of William's by the interstate, I guess that's why we only seen each other at school. My husband was still at work when my son went to his friend house. When my son got there, they were getting ready for supper. His friend parents were in the kitchen, and his friend took him in to introduce to them. When his friend said dad this is my new friend from school as he turn around from the sink, my son seen his father with another family. He immediately asked is father how could you do this? Especially to my mother, who loves you with her whole heart and soul, and you do have other children at home. I thought I would remind you, just in case you forgot. Who are these people, and what are you doing here? So I guess this is your other family, and this is why you can't attend any of my school activities. So this is your overtime, and is spent over here not on your job. Then his dad came toward him to explain, what was going on. My son ran out the door, and he continued to run all the way home without stopping. When he got home, he was crying, screaming, and disturb. I tried to calm him down; he looked at me and said mom our father is living a double life. I asked my son, what do you mean? He began to explain everything to me. Am I a Damaged Woman? Yes I am.

Here is something else I know happens all the time. You have a best friend and no one can pull you two apart. Then one day you finally get married, and your friend is still single. She sees how happy you are, and she has never had happiness like that. You always trusted her around your husband because she is your best friend. One day she decides she needs to be happy, because she sees what she is missing in her life. Instead of letting love find her, she figure she have found love in her best friend husband. The reason why she feels this way is because she spends the majority of her time with him. So one day she tells him she can make him happier than his wife. I need you to remember this is her best friend from childhood. As we know how weak some men are, as she was saying this they was at his house while his wife was at work. He got so caught up in the moment until he forgot where he was. Then they engaged in a kiss one thing lead to another soon they were in bed. That day his wife decides to surprise him by coming home early from work. She didn't call him like she usually does she just left from work. On her way home she was full of joy, thinking how lucky she was just to have a great husband. She was just singing their favorite song, and continually saying my husband is going to be so surprise, because he don't know we will be going on a cruise. Its called Couples in Love cruise, and I won two tickets everything paid. So she finally arrive to the house being very quiet, with the tickets in her hand. All the lights were still on but her husband was upstairs. She tipped up the stairs as she got closer to the room by the door way she scream surprise, still holding the tickets in her hand. Only the surprise was on her, she immediately drops the tickets, because what she had seen. Her best friend from their childhood in bed with her husband. Then she remembered my mother used to say don't let your best friend be around your husband or wife all the time, because those are the ones who will take them from you. It's much easier for them to do it than a stranger is, because those are the ones you trust. Am I a Damaged Woman? Yes I am.

This is a little F.Y.I. (for your information) for all the ladies if you are thinking about seeing a married man. Don't forget what he did to his wife to be with you. It's the same man, same liar, same tricks, and you are the next damaged woman. I just want to give you something to think about. He also told his wife he loved her.

Can you image something like that happening to you? This is something we do as jealous people all the time. We are not happy and we don't want to see know one else happy. I don't care what people say I know misery do love company. That's why we do all we can do to destroy someone else's life. We got to have what other people have this is called envy. We need to be ourselves and stop trying to be like others. That's why so many homes are broken up, and so much crime is going on, because we are without Christ is in our lives. We don't care about others just ourselves. When will we start to care? Probably when it involves our family and we start to hurt.

You know what can be as Damaging as if you went through the ordeal yourself. Is that you find out that your husband sexually molested all of your children, and has been doing it for years. What's so bad about it you didn't have a clue it was going on. Until one day one of your daughters became pregnant, and she had to tell whom the father of her child was. Then they all confess of the horrible thing, that has been going on since they can remember. What about the times they can't remember, so how long has this been going on? Was I too blind to see what was happening in my own house? Was I to involved in other things? I didn't take the time to save my own children from terror. All this time I was in the dark, in my house now. What do I do to get rid of this fungus out of my children lives? I need help I can't handle this thing by myself. But how can a father do this to his own children? He is suppose to protect them from harm not harm them. Am I a Damaged Woman? Yes I am.

I don't understand how people make the innocent their target, is it because it's so easy? Maybe the reason for that is they're not real men, especially when they can't face their own fears. Why can't we just seek help for our problems, instead of taking them out on the weak? That is really a coward mentality. We have some woman that is so damaged they just refuse to trust men.

This is something that happens all the time. You have shacked up with this man for about fifteen years. You have four children for him, and he has never married you. This man comes and goes when it pleases him with no question asked. He's out when you are home trying to take care of his four children. You want to get married, but he keeps saying he's not ready. If you're not ready after fifteen years and four children you will never be ready. Then you start hearing people talk about your man cheating on you. Finally what people are saying about him comes true. Your man has married a woman who doesn't have any children for him. This is truly a very damaged woman. Some men just have that kind of nerves, and don't care who gets hurt.

Then we have the ones who don't know they are damaged women. Their husbands don't let them associate with anyone but him. If they have a job he comes and pick up the check. They are scared to say no to their husband, because they're afraid of what he might say. He doesn't allow you to "think for yourself he tells you what to do." They can't talk to their families or go visit them. This man has you in bondage that's not love its control. The minute someone calls you he changes your phone number. When someone finds out where you live you just up and move. Your children don't know anyone that's related to them. That's very dangerous what is he hiding, and wouldn't you like too know? There are some women when they go shopping they hide what they buy. This is still bondage, because you don't have an opened and honest relationship.

I understand there are different ways of being a Damage Woman, and women have many ways of being hurt. Domestic violence is one of the most leading causes of a Damage Woman. Statistics "show if abuse woman don't seek help it leads to death." When someone are abusing you, they don't love you. What they are doing is killing you slowly. We are not supposed to be afraid of the people that say they love us. I tell people all the time love doesn't hurt, because when you love someone you don't hurt them. When two people are married they become one. So whatever you do to one it should have an affect on the other. You need to know that being afraid to tell, want save your life. Ladies there are shelters in every state that you can turn too. So stop staying and start praying for a way to get free. Try to find that one person you know you can trust I the time of trouble.

Also if you are being stalk by someone, that's very damaging. Everywhere you go you see them, and all they do is just stare at you. He's outside your house, grocery store, job, and just everywhere you go. You can't sleep, eat, can't do your job right anymore, but yet you are afraid to tell. Just think if all this happen to you when you were in your youth. Growing up with all the hurt and pain. In a very difficult situation, you don't know whom you can trust or who to turn to for help.

You live this nightmare not knowing what tomorrow will bring. As you become a teenager the nightmare still there. When you become a young adult the nightmare is still there. When you become an adult the nightmare is still there. Now you are on your own, what is going to take place because the nightmare is still there? Remember you never told anyone because you were afraid. So how do you live a normal life, knowing you don't trust people? You have relationships after relationships neither one of them lasting. You're looking for love that you didn't get as a child. You haven't dealt with your childhood fears yet. You're trying to find someone who would take care of you. Someone to love you, depend on, talk to, and someone you can trust, and not worry about. If I lye down and close my eyes, will I be violated? This is something that is still with you and it's hard to get pass not knowing how to handle your fears. This is truly a life-damaging thing; just to know how some people are filled with uncontrollable spirits. This happens to people all the time all over the world, and it's time we do something about it.

We have good spirits and bad spirits, and we cannot control them ourselves. For instance, the crack addict, the desire is uncontrollable. He or she can't break the habit on their own, and the rehab room can't seem to do it either. Whenever they leave the room their addiction starts calling their name. The alcoholic the desire for alcohol is just to great, it looks like the habit is too hard to break. The same with smoking no matter how hard I try I just can't quit. I quit three times already, and I always start back. Wake up with one, one before I start work. One or two when I go on a ten minute break. Can somebody tell me how he or she quit smoking? What about the gambling habit? I'm losing all my money, pawning everything, selling everything, and getting loans. Just to soothe my gambling addiction. There's a 1(800) get- help number on billboards all across America. What can I do, I just can't quit? Well I tell you method I know is sure to work it's call 1(800) seek-God.

Matthew 6: 33 states, But seek ye first the kingdom God, and his righteousness ad all these things will be added unto to you.

Everybody wants to know how they can handle a life unexpected situation. Just to let everyone know who wants to give up, there is still hope. For any difficult task that you are going through there's yet a way out. I learned that just for being in the right place, at the right time. Let me tell you about this place. It's a little Church on a dead-end street, called the church of Love. The church taught, and I learn how to trust and believe in God. How God is in control of everyone and everything. Without him nothing is possible, no matter what we say or do. We need God in our lives in order for us to be humble. Just to know that we can go to God in prayer and during prayer burdens are lifted. I didn't know this was possible, until I committed myself in going to church.

At first when I start going to the church I didn't receive anything, because I was always worrying about the time, and how long church was lasting. When I realized I needed help like yesterday, I got busy learning more about God. I started reading more, and it became a habit. I had a new habit I was learning more about God addiction. I did exactly that I got in the word then the word got in me. I began to see a difference in myself and in other people. I wasn't as negative as I use to be. I got involved in different departments in the church. I learned how to forgive my brother, love, respect, how to live holy, trust, and believed that Jesus is the way, truth, and the life. I acknowledge that Jesus paid it all, he was wounded and crucified for all sin.

Psalms 121:1-2 states, I will lift up mine eyes unto the hills, from whence cometh my help.

2 My help cometh from the Lord, which made heaven and earth.

Just knowing you can make it, and everything will be all right. It really makes you feel good knowing there's help. I didn't know these things at first. By going to church and learning more about God the better understanding I got about God and life.

Just to know in *2 Corinthians 12:9 Jesus states; My grace is sufficient for thee: for my strength is made perfect in weakness*

I didn't know what that meant, until I really start learning more about God. Going to Sunday school, morning service, ypww in the evening, and night service. We also had Wednesday night service, which was Bible study. As the lesson went forth, a lot of times they would compare it to everyday life. Some of the lesson was unbelievable you had to ask yourself did this really happen? They really suffered a lot, especially Job. Many of times I would ask myself, why did all these horrible things always happen to me? As I continued to go to church I learned, and I found out why. Then I started seeking God each day, reading my Bible I became more knowledgeable about understanding difficult situation, and how to get pass them.

Matthew 11:28-30 states; Come unto me, all ye that labour and are heavy laden, and I will give you rest.

***29 Take my yoke upon you, and learn of me; for
I am meek and lowly in heart: and ye shall find rest
unto your souls.***

30 For my yoke is easy, and my burden is light.
From reading, teaching, learning, and applying it to
my life, I have changed for the better. It's letting me
know that all things are possible. You can really make
a difference in your own life. You can hold your head
up high, just believe there is hope. You can become
someone who can make a difference in someone else's
life also. That's why I know now no matter how many
Rehab sit down session you have, if you don't seek God
for deliverance you will always carry the unwanted
burdens. Which can lead to suicide, bad relationship,
never forgiving, not trusting anyone, and just never
happy with yourself or anyone else. I learned from
attending all the church services that God can heal
all wounds, and all habits, if you just give it to him
and leave them all with him. The teaching, preaching,
and the studying of God's word, bring you closer and
closer in his presence. Your prayer life become ordi-
nary then fasting begin. You will begin fasting and
praying. God will soon bring all things back to your
remembrance whether good or bad. You will begin to
understand where you should go from there. I needed

to start accepting those things I could not change, and move forward with God being the head of my life. Just have faith that he will make everything all right. The Bible tells us in *Hebrews 11:6 But without faith it is impossible to please him; for he that cometh to God must believe that he is, and that he is a rewarder of them that diligently seek him.*

So I'm encouraging you to seek Him because no matter what you have been through, God can bring you out. That's certainly without a doubt, he can make it all right for you. Just to know Him as your personal Saviour makes the load much lighter. I know now, that I can't conquer any bad situations without Him. I have learned how to lean, and depend on Jesus for help, strength, belief, endurance, faith and more faith.

Revelation 3:20-21 states, Behold, I stand at the door, and knock: if any man hear my voice, and open the door, I will come into him, and will sup with him, and he with me.

21 To him that over come it will I grant to sit with me in my throne, even as I also overcame, and am set with my Father in his throne.

Just knowing someday I will get the crown of life, and God telling me well done my good and faithful servant. In order to make it to Heaven forgiveness is also important.

Galatians 6:7-9; Be not deceived; God is not mocked: for whatsoever a man soweth, that shall he also reap.

8 For he that soweth to the flesh shall of the flesh reap corruption; but he that soweth to the spirit shall of the spirit reap life everlasting.

9And let us not be weary in well doing: for in due season we shall reap, if we faint not.

Just knowing if we give ourselves to God and except Him in our hearts He will take care of us.

He said we would reap the benefits if we faint not. I know this is a fact because he did it for me. God help me get pass the hurt, loneliness, disgrace, and all the bad feelings I had inside, and wanting to kill for what happen to me growing up, I was only fourteen years old, and again I was sixteen. I wasn't aware of what life was about; I didn't know why someone would do this to another person. Lord I thank you for coming into my heart one day, and saving me before it was too late. I was one of those people who had relationships that didn't last because I didn't trust men. Oh but when I gave it totally to God. My desire is to be all that I can be for God in these last and evil days. I might not be the best, but I'm doing my best to make things right. I will walk right, talk right, and live right so other people can be delivered from their damage situation. I can let my light so shine before men, that they may see my good works, and glorify my Father, which is in Heaven. That way they can also give God their bad situations.

Being a Damage Woman is not a good thing. Especially if you grew up with the problem, and still holding on to it and not trying to get help for it. It's time for you to let Jesus fix it for you and let him be your guide. He will not lead you down the wrong path. The Lord can be your shepherd, and he will lead you to being righteous for his namesake. Get in the word of God and he will give you peace, joy, love, hope, happiness, understanding and much more, just give him a chance. There's nothing like it, I tell you, having peace with yourself is a wonderful experience. You will feel so good about everything, and just having peace in your soul, makes a difference. You will want everybody that you come in contact with, to know how good God is. I know it will take time, because it didn't happen overnight for me. I carried unwanted baggage for a long time with me. One day I was driving and God spoke to me and said you know I forgive

why can't you? From that day on I started seeking
more and more on how to forgive those whom had
took advantage of me. Was it easy? No it wasn't, but
with God it got much easier each day.

The other stories weren't mines, but these are. The
other stories were people I met along the way when
I was going through my bad situation. I want you
to "know every two minutes someone is being rape,
murdered, shot, abused, neglected, or divorced." I'm
going to try and tell you what situations God has
made easier for me to handle. I'm going to let you
know what God help me to understand. I grew up in
my grandparent's house. I don't know if they knew
how to say I love you, if so I never heard them say it.
They discipline us thoroughly, sometimes I thought
too much. I guess they did the best they knew how. I
came to the conclusion the reason our grandparents
were so hard on us, because they didn't want us to
be like our mother. Every year our mother was drop-
ping of another baby on them. When you are raising
someone else's children it's not an easy job. My mother
had a good friend in Arkansas, who sometimes was
the baby-sitter for my younger sisters and brothers.
She had sons and no daughters, she was supposed to

be a friend, her and her children. They was just like our other family, we was always together.

My mother had seven girls and three boys at that time; later she had another boy total of eleven children living. We were friends; at least I thought we were someone who you can run to in the time of trouble. We was always told if someone bothers us, tell somebody we know. One night I was at my friend's house not knowing I was in trouble, because I was safe there, at my friends house. As I was sitting there the friends I knew from first grade, one put his hand over my mouth, one grabbed my legs, one grabbed my arms, and one start pulling my clothes off. I couldn't imagine what they were doing, I was never taught by anyone about sex. My friends held me down and rape me all night repeatedly. They laugh as they put themselves in side of me. Even though I screamed and cried out they continue to hold my mouth so no one can hear me. I know for a fact this lady knew what her children were doing, and she looked the other way. It takes a poor mother not to know what going own in her home. My very own friends stole my child hood from me. If you can't trust your child hood friends, whom can you trust? The ones I used to make mud pies with. We used to jump rope together.

Played dodge ball during recess and lunch period. I couldn't imagine them doing something like this to me. I never would have guessed this in a million years. Who do we really know? I hope they are not engaging in making others life miserable. I hope they repented for what they done to me. As I begin to type about what happen that night I started thinking to myself that "they could have killed me." I could have been cut up and left for dead. I will continue to say whom do we really know? The answer is nobody. I was also rape when I was six months pregnant by a very close friend of our family. I was in my bed sleeping I didn't know he was in the house. This man rapes me and didn't care if I was pregnant. Who do we know? The answer is nobody. The reasons I "say nobody is because people who you think are good people are really not good people." When a woman is six months pregnant she can't defend herself. I just stop trusting in people in general. When I twenty-five I made a mistake with a young man. He got very anger when I ended the relationship and started stalking me. I went to the authorities, and all they did was talk to him and let him go. He continued stalking me I couldn't sleep, think, and I couldn't function with this happening to me. Everywhere I turn he was there, no peace at all. Until one day he decided to go his own way. I was so glad when he finally left me alone. Two years went by I became involved with someone I thought I knew. Baby I'm here to tell you I didn't know him at all. He became a stalker also; again I went to the authorities many of times. They said they couldn't do him anything because he had not committed a crime. I ask the Deputy what is he supposed to do kill me first? Then one night I moved to a different location without anyone knowing. About one year later we cross paths again, and he told me he was sorry. I still didn't trust him and I didn't let my guard down. Even though I went through those ordeals, it's still nothing like being held hostage all night and being misused. They were not concern about what they were putting me through. The only thing they were concern about was how they felt. Back when I was growing up you couldn't talk to your family or friends about anything. Whenever someone did tell they were called a lie, and weren't believed. When I was growing up they didn't have rape kits or DNA swabs. It wouldn't do you any good to tell because they would call you a lie, and they wouldn't take you to the hospital. "I know in the back of their mind that they knew it was true." Maybe the woman was just that terrified of the male figure, because they couldn't do any thing unless the man said yes. You also had those women that did know, but was too afraid to say anything. One reason why they were afraid because their husbands would leave them and there would be no one to provide for them. Another reason is that it would have brought shame to their families. That's why they had a lot of hidden stuff no one knew about. Let me "tell you about some of those things I call hidden stuff. You couldn't find many women that would tell on her husband. He probably would beat her down every night and no one knew, because she kept it a secret. When a child got pregnant she was pull out of school before she would begin to show. After the child was born the mother was forced to tell the child they were siblings. The mother would have a deaf ear to her child being molested. Now a day you find some woman with a backbone. I "say with friction back in the day the woman wasn't allowed to voice her opinion." The majority of woman took the hand that was dealt. This is why our children feel like they are nothing, because of the disbelief, and the silence. This is why our children try to kill themselves. I know this because I tried to end my life at a young age. There are some kids that tried to tell, and no one would listen. It is a bad thing when the parents destroy their own children.

I thank God for sparing my life and giving me another chance. If God had not given me another chance I wouldn't be able to help someone with my story. I was also in an abusive marriage in 1988. From the minute I said I do my first husband change, it was like night and day. He started saying he was older than I was, and I will do what he says. He said I'm the man I'm in control of the house, and everything you do. Then one day he decided to throw a punch to my face. I can't fight two or three people at one time but one on one I can really deliver. You can believe me whenever the man get the nerve to hit you that one time it's an ongoing thing. He said he was sorry, but it didn't stop we stayed fighting. The reason I say we were fighting, because I fought back ladies. Then one day I woke up, and I decided that wasn't the life for me. I didn't want to be fighting all the time all bruised up with my body aching. It was on a Sunday evening when he came home drunk making a lot of noise about nothing. We got into an argument he slap me and walked into the bathroom. I didn't hit him back that day, because my mind was made the next time he hit me it's over. So I grabbed my purse, and I went next door and called the Police. When the Police got there they heard both sides of the story. Then I showed the police the bruise on my face, and they escorted him away from the house. I was delivered from that marriage, and all it's problems. About five years later after the divorce he died from alcohol. Only until years later when I was able to understand, in order for God to heal my broken heart, I had to give him all the pieces. We all have trials to go through, some seem worst than others but if we just keep the faith, we will overcome them. Having hate, malice, unforgiving and dislike is sin, this can only weigh you down, it's so heavy you can barely walk with this infirmity.

Luke 13:10-13 states; And he was teaching in one of the synagogues on the sabbath.

11 And behold, there was a woman which had a spirit of infirmity eighteen years, and was bowed together, and could in no wise lift up herself.

12 And when Jesus saw her, he called her to him, and said unto her, Woman, thou art loosed from thine infirmity.

13And he laid his hands on her: and immediately she was made straight, and glorified God.

God loosed her and she glorified him. God delivered me and I'm glad about it. Whatever happened in your life and you think you can't bare it, try God and I guarantee you he will help you through all your trials and tribulation. He will give you a new way of thinking he can free your mind of all debris. You can get help so you can get stronger in order to help someone else. We all can't be defeated; someone has to be strong. The enemy is still lurking in the daylight, darkness, and wherever he can find a victim.

1 Peter 5:8 Be sober, be vigilant; because your adversary the devil, as a roaring lion, walketh about, seeking whom he may devour:

Daddies are raping their daughters and sons, and their children are afraid to tell anyone. Friends you know and people you don't know are still committing these awful acts. We need to get help for them, while we are helping them it will also help us. We don't just have Damage Woman; we also have Damage Men. They didn't know whom to talk to either, that's why they don't come forth until someone else does. By them holding their problems in for a long time, that's how they became predators. The same applies to you also, no matter what you think; God can deliver you from that bad situation.

"I tell my co-workers all the time, no matter how it looked the first time you looked at it, look at it again." All

things are possible with God no matter what you are going through. God can loose you and you can glorify him to. Wherever there's a need God can fix it. He can heal all your wounds and give you your joy back. First you need help with the childhood problems.

I remember long time ago; I would hear grown folks say to their children don't talk to strangers. They would tell them if any one tried to touch them that they didn't know, run and scream for help. They would also say don't take anything from strangers, and don't get in the car with strangers. Yes we need to be concern about strangers, and we don't need to put our full trust in them. Strangers is really not the problem, it's the ones we know as our family members and friends. Yes we still have strangers lurking and we need to be aware. It's not the people we know as outsiders; it's the people on the inside we need to be afraid of. Everyone who violated me I knew them, they weren't strangers. We think we know people but we really don't. We are sleeping with the enemy in the next room, next door, up the street, and behind us. Fathers are molesting and raping their sons and daughters. Mothers are doing the same they are killing their own children. Pornography is put on the web site of children, they are lured to different states and being rape and murdered. It's called *my space* is the number one way to lure children. The only way your underage child can talk on *my space* is to have access to you identification. How can you trust someone you can't see or never met? You can barely trust the ones you are around all the time. Parents please don't let your daughters be another damage woman or your sons a damage man.

Especially Priest, I have never seen any statement saying a priest couldn't or shouldn't get married.

Proverbs 18:22 Whoso findeth a wife findeth a good thing, and obtaineth favour of the Lord.

1Corinthians 7:1-2, Now concerning the things whereof ye wrote unto me: It is good for a man not to touch a woman.

2 Nevertheless, to avoid fornication, let every man have his own wife, and let every woman have her own husband.

1 Corinthians 7: 7-9, For I would that all men even as I myself. But every man hath his proper gift of God, one after this manner, ands another after that.

8 I say therefore to the unmarried and widows, It is good for them if they abide even as I.

9 But if they cannot contain, let them marry: for it is better to marry than to burn.

There's no where in the Bible stating a man shouldn't marry. Just admit you are a rapist and ask God to forgive you. Denounce your priesthood, and repent so you can move on with your life. How can you keep a secret like that? Especially when you are hearing everyone else's confession. Sitting in the confession booth is not going to save you. The only one you a fooling is yourself, because you haven't been delivered. I say this, because every chance you get you rapes again. Then you confess again; you just repeating the cycle aren't you?

Leviticus 20:13 If man also lie with mankind, as he lieth with a woman, both of them have committed an abomination: they shall surely be put to death; their blood shall be upon them.

Paul adored God that's why he was able to sustain and keep himself. If you are not a true man of God he will uncover your sins. The filthy things you are containing in your mind, soul, spirit, and flesh. Paul states if you can't keep yourself go find you a wife. He didn't say go and be a child molester. It's time to get it right, and stop pretending it's all right.

Teachers sleeping with their students you are a pedophile. It's time for you to seek God, get help, repent, and admit that you are a child molester.

Doctors, Lawyers, Preachers, Football players, *Mayors, Teachers, Fireman, Policeman, Basketball players*, and I don't need to go on you know who you are. People are doing it and getting away with it. So tell me who is the stranger and whom do we run to? Sinful flesh and uncontrollable spirits are all around us, so who do we trust with our lives? God is still healing people's mind, body, and soul. If you let God, He can see you through any and all past experience. It doesn't matter if we don't trust anybody else, we can always trust God, and He's not a stranger. God can never be a stranger unless we let him be.

It goes back to *Revelation 3:20 Behold, I stand at the door, and knock: if any man hear my voice, and open the door, I will come in to him, and will sup with him, and he with me.*

So how can God be a stranger, he's asking us to let him in, because he wants to take care of us. What ever we need God's got it, and He wants to share it with us. If you need relief from your pain now I know whom you can run to, and be safe. We need to learn, love, and live. Learn by reading God's word, and understanding it. *Matthew 24:35 states, Heaven and earth shall pass away, but my words shall not pass away.* So you can stand on the word of God knowing that every word is true. Hearing, believing, and applying his word to our lives. Love, Gods people by treating them like you treat yourself. Loving and obeying his word to become a better person. Live like a born again believer, by applying his word to our life.

2 Corinthians 5:17 states Therefore if any man be in Christ, he is a new creature: old things are passed away; behold, all things are become new.

Everything about you change it don't stay the same. You will have a new way of walking, a new way of talking, a new way of thinking, and a new way of looking at life. As I stated before I could have got revenge by killing or doing something else that would have got me in serious trouble. I truly thank God for coming into my life when he did.

Hebrews 10:30 states; For we know him that said, Vengeance belongeth unto me, I will recompense, saith the Lord. And again, the Lord shall judge his people.

Romans 12:19 states; Dearly beloved, avenge not yourselves, but rather give place unto wrath:

for it is written, Vengeance is mine; I will repay,
saith the Lord.

God is telling us no matter what happen he is still
in control. Just when you think there's no hope, if you
give it to him he will fix that bad situation for you.
You don't have to lift a finger, get in his word you will
understand it better by and by. God is the only one
I can give my problems to, and he will make them
much easier to bare. Many times we tell people our
problems or they know what happen to us. They try
to reassure you it's going to be all right. Only until
you walk in the same shoes that someone else has
walked in, it's difficult for you to know what they are
going through. If you don't know how to make brown
gravy, how can you teach me. That's like me going to
someone who is single to help me with my marriage.
Someone who has never been married can't help you
with your marriage, because they don't know what to
tell you. If you never been on drugs you don't know
what to tell a drug attic, or a recovering attic. If you
never been homeless, what can you tell the one's that
is sleeping on the street. If we have been through bad
situation, we can share with someone else in order to
help someone them. Let it our job to make others life
easier. We can also help others with our testimony.

Revelation 12:11 And they overcame him by the blood of the Lamb, and by the words of their testimony.

The more we share our past experience with others it will also help us deal with our problems better. Sometimes we have to go through trials and tribulations to make us what we are, and to keep us strong. Until we figure this out, we will always be weak. I often wonder why did all these things happen to me. Just think if it had not happen, I wouldn't be writing this book in order to help someone else. I've learned how to go through, because when we try to fix things ourselves all we do is mess things up. If I had took matters in my hands I would have been writing this behind bars, not in my den. Even though trouble come our way we are not the only ones who have been through trying times. There were many people in the Bible days that really went through some trials.

Matthew 9: 20 states And, behold, a woman, which was diseased with an issue of blood for twelve years, came behind him, and touch the hem of his garment.

No doubt there were people everywhere, because Jesus was on his way to a certain rulers house to raise his daughter from the dead. I can imagine people were everywhere, and by it being so many you couldn't see Jesus because they were surrounding him. I know the woman with the issue had to be weak from losing all that blood for all those years. Oh but when she heard that Jesus was about to pass that way, she got enough strength to make her way there, in order to be healed. She might have been crawling we don't' t know, but we do know she made her way to Jesus.

Matthew 9:21 For she said within herself, If I may but touch his garment, I shall be made whole.

We also know that Jesus told her in ***Matthew 9:22 Daughter, be of good comfort; thy faith hath made thee whole***.

If I had to preach that right now my thought would be, *keep pressing for your blessing*. Whatever situation you are going through that you can't fix, it doesn't matter what it is God can fix it. No one can say they suffered like Jesus did, and be able to handle it. Many of us can't handle a paper cut. Jesus himself went through some terrible trials and never said a mumbling word. He just suffered in order to make things good for us to see his Father. After he done all he could do to save those, which was lost we still turn our back on him.

When Jesus was in Gethsemane, he said, ***O my Father, if it possible, let this cup pass from me: nevertheless not as I will, but as thou wilt. Matthew 26:39.*** Jesus said nevertheless, meaning I will do whatever has to be done. I will go and pave the way, and do what ever is necessary to save my people. Can we say that we would have done this just to help others? We are to busy looking out for ourselves, we don't have time to help someone else.

Jesus knew he had to go to the cross, in order for his people to have the right to the tree of life. Jesus was done in a way we will never imagine. So I thank God for letting me live through all my heartaches and pain. Now I'm here to help where I can, until we get our hearts right and except Jesus as our Lord and Saviour, we will never be able to help anyone else. There will always be a violator waiting to prey on the innocent. That's when we need to be strong, because we know what the weak are going through, and that's when they need our help. It is much easier for someone to talk about a bad situation; if the person they are talking to been through the same ordeal no matter how horrific it was. Just being there for someone can make the difference between life and death. Everyone is not strong enough to seek God but for the ones that is, let's try to help the ones that's not able. Everyday something strange happens. Even when someone is convicted for a child molestation crime, they are sent to therapy and just because they tell the therapist what they want to hear, they figure they are cured. Just as soon as they get released, and they come in contact with children old feelings come back, and they are back to molesting children. While they were locked up they seem to be cured because they were not around children, so you couldn't get a good diagnosis. There is a difference when you can and can't get to something, the difference is as long as it's not around you it has no affect on you. As soon as you come in contact with it the table changes. The uncontrollable spirit over takes them, and they can't control themselves. They also have to be careful about what they watch on television. The television shows they are showing now are just unreal. People are enjoying as they watch movies, where both genders are being rape. If you are going to watch a show like this, you need to watch one where they are solving crimes like these. People with weak minds don't need to watch shows like that, because they will soon try to act this out. Or it will be a reminder to the ones who already have done this horrible act. It don't matter what the television show, being rape is not something you enjoy. As I stated before some people never get over the torment, and their mental state never comes back. So tell me what kind of life is this to live? Not a good one especially when you don't trust nobody. This is why we need God in our lives, he's standing at the door, how many times do he need to knock? Before you answer you need to know it's impossible to defeat the devil by yourself.

James 4:7 states; Submit yourselves therefore to God. Resist the devil, and he will flee from you. Many times we ask the question, how can we resist? This is all I know, and all I seen growing up as a child. If all you seen were smoking, drinking, and drugs going on in your house, you figure this is the right thing to do, unless you are told different. Same way with abuse, you think this is the thing to do. Many people have this excuse, my daddy did it, my grandfather did it and they go on and on talking about the people in their family who did whatever. Then they start saying it's a generation curse that's hogwash. Is it a thing as a generation curses? If so is its time for that curse to be broken. Someone needs to take a stand and say, "I will not be like the curse generation. "The problem is, that's all you seen growing up and you figure that's the thing to do because you were not told not to do it, and it was wrong.

You never had any sense of directions and were never, "told if you give that problem to God he can make it all right." You never knew he could break all curses if you would just give it to him. It's time to glorify God for being loosed, from all your infirmities, someone need to testify that God did it for me to. Don't forget when you are down to nothing, God is up to something. I learned over the year that is a true saying. All those times I thought I wasn't going to make it, some how God always brought me out. I'm reminded there is a light at the end of the tunnel, no matter how dark it looks. Just keep holding on and you can make it, whatever you do don't give up.

There's a bright side somewhere, just keep looking until you find it. Look until you find a true friend, you don't have to look far, just call him, he'll be there. When you can't talk to no one else you can always talk to God, he's just a prayer away. Never feel like you are defeated, that's how the devil want you to feel. You need to know whom you can turn to. Just remember ***Psalms 121:1-2 states; I will lift up mine eyes unto the hill, from whence cometh my help.***

2 *My help cometh from the Lord, which made heaven and earth*.

Just keep looking up, knowing nothing is to hard for my God to handle. Once you understand that everything is possible with God you can move on with your life in a positive way. Keep trying as hard as you can to do what's right. By being on the Lord side you can't go wrong. We need our minds healed totally in order to move forward. As I stated once before until I gave my mind, body, and soul to God I was not able to understand what it was I needed to do to get my life back. I can't stress it enough man can't heal the soul only God can. There's not enough therapy in the whole entire world that can heal the soul. I let Jesus fix for me one day and he did just that. I gave all my problems to God, and let me tell you he did for me. One day one of my friends told me you will never meet anyone nice, because all you do is go to work and church then back home. She stated and you know you don't have any men go to your church. I told her, you know what I'm not looking for anyone I'm trying to find myself. I needed to get things right with myself first, at that time I was really in to God delivering me from my infirmities. I couldn't have another relationship at that time if I wanted to, because I knew it wouldn't work, so why waste my time and his. I wasn't ready for that kind of problem yet, all I was doing at that time was getting closer to God so I can finally get my life back on the right track. Everyday I was getting older and older then I "thought to myself it's time for me to do the right thing. I heard the messages go forth it was time for me to make a move. I heard the message **get right church and let's go home**. I heard the message get back satan I'm running late. I will not capitalize satan, only my God come with a capital G and my Jesus come with a capital J. they are bigger than any problem I ever had. I knew I had to **Get Over It,** and move on. I knew I had to stop holding on to old stuff. That was one of the reasons I couldn't move on. Many times we ask God to deliver us, but we hold on to the problems instead of letting them go. We know how we compare everything to our first marriage, even though the marriage been over. I said I don't know if I will ever get married again. I didn't say I wouldn't get married again, there was a lady told me a long time ago. She said don't ever say what you'll not going to do, because you don't know what you will do before you leave from this earth. She also said don't ever say who you want need, because the one you say you doesn't need. God will make everybody you go to shut his or her door in your face and will send you back to the one you said you didn't need. I just said, "if I were delivered out of this marriage I would know what to do the next time." Over the years I learned more and more about God, and how he can deliver me and give me my joy back. One Sunday we were having a great church service we had a speaker from out of town. After he finish he had an altar call for those whom needed prayer. We all need prayer so I went for prayer. When it was time for him to pray for me, he told me that God told him to tell me he was going to send me a husband, so I say yes right and politely and went and sit down, I didn't wait until he finish praying for me. Someone ask me one day did I think God would give us what we need to stay save? Little did I know something was getting ready to happen to me? I was getting ready to make a difference in my life and in others. Would you believe what the Preacher told me at the altar came true? It's been eleven years look at God, he is in control. I have learned over the years that everything happen is meant to happen. I 'm really serving God, all I know how and if I slip in anyway I make sure I repent, because nobody on earth is perfect. We are striving for perfection, to do the things that are pleasing in God's sight. ***God loosed*** *me and I glorify Him* for who He is, and what He has done in my life. He came in and made a big difference; I have no problems with forgiven now. I'm not the same person I use to be I'm able to say if you need my help just let me know. When you can say I know that I can make it now, you will feel so much better about living. No more suicide thought, no more wishing you wasn't born, no more holding your head down, no more low self esteem, no more hiding in the house, no more crying all the time, no more just letting yourself go, just don't care what you look like. I want you to know that forgive you, and you don't win. You had me bound for a long time, but I'm free now. *Its time out for being bound let's break the chains that's holding us down.* It's time for us to take control of our own lives, and stop letting the devil think he has defeated us. It's time for him to go back to the pits of hell where he belongs. We need to start opening our mouths and claiming our healing and deliverance right now. We need to get enough courage to start rebuking the devil out loud. We are stronger than we think we are; we just need to put forth the effort so we can be healed. We as women and men can all "say at the same time I need a healing. Its nothing like being free from bad situation, when you turn it over to Jesus it will be all right.

John 8:36 states; If the son therefore shall make you free, ye shall be free indeed.

Just knowing you can be free makes a difference, all you have to say is yes Lord. It's time to say I surrender all to you, here I am Lord take full control of me. Then you can stand and see the salvation of the Lord take place in your life. You can see what good things the Lord has in store for you, and you will be able to share with others about your new experience. Then you can believe that God is who he says he is. Once you let him deliver you out of your bondage. You know it is one thing to know of God. Oh, but it's another thing to know him. Just to have that personal relationship with him. You will be able to stand back and see the red sea open for you, and you will also see Pharaoh's army being defeated, because you have the victory in Christ Jesus. Just being in the path of God will bring great things your way. Yes you will still have some trials, but they only come to make you strong. As we know we can handle those trials much easier now with Christ. In order to build up, you have to tare down every once in awhile. This only makes us stronger to be a good support holder. If you never go through a storm, how do you know if you can weather it? It's impossible to have faith if you never had a faith tester. I tell everybody I've gone through the fire, and I've been through the flood, my heart have been torn all to pieces, I think I have seen it all, but now I can say I still have joy. I will continual to praise God anyhow. Why? Because through it all God brought me out of darkness into his marvelous light, and I'm glad about it. I'm no longer afraid to "tell people with God I'm able to handle any bad situation. I understand very well now what God can do, and I know every word he say is true. Maybe by us knowing this, we can help the ones that's preying on the weak change his or her life to become a believer. All things are possible with and through God. All we have to do is put it in his hand, and he will do the rest. God has healed the sick, raise the dead, made the blind too see, the lame to walk, he has healed the leper it doesn't stop there, nothing is to hard for God if you just believe he can do it. All God wants you to do is to repent for your sins.

1 John 1: 9 states, If we confess our sins, he is faithful and just to forgive us our sins, and to cleanse us from all unrighteousness.

I want you to know he will clean you up, because he did it for me. I want everyone to know what he done for me, and I'm not ashamed to tell the truth.

John 8:32 states, And ye shall know the truth, and the truth shall make you free.

The truth is," in order for God to forgive us we have to forgive others."

Matthew 6:14-15 states, For if ye forgive men their trespasses, your heavenly Father will also forgive you:

15 But if ye forgive not men their trespasses, neither will your Father forgive your trespasses.

We have to know if you turn your life over to God, he will make your life brand new, and you will forget that thing ever happen. This is something you can't do yourself. Many people say they have to get right before they go to church, but this is something you can't do yourself only God can fix you, but you have to have your mind made up. Jesus has laid the foundation and open up the way. Whenever you go to church, you have to go with your heart open to hear the word of God in order for it to take root. You can't worry about what others think, you need to be delivered from your infirmities, and only God can deliver you. God will put you in a place with yourself that you have never been before in your life. It's something whenever you try to describe it and you can't explain it. All you can say is that I'm at peace with myself. When you talk to your friends, and they ask you how and why you look so different? You will say, "God did it". One thing about people they will notice you no matter if you are looking good or bad. Once you start going in the right direction it's easy to take the right path. You have to do what's right in order to stay on the right path. So you will have to have a good path leader.

Proverbs 3:5-6 states, Trust in the Lord with all thine heart; and lean not unto thine own understanding.

6 In all thy ways acknowledge him, and he shall direct thy path.

I know I'm making it sound so easy now, it is easy now but at the beginning it wasn't, but now it is. Why do I say that? ***God loosed me and I glorify him*** for coming into my life at the right time. I can tell you over and over again what he has done for me, and you might or might not believe me. I challenge you to try him for yourself and I guarantee you, you will be trying to get in touch with me to tell me he did the same thing for you. What a good feeling knowing you can live again, and be free of past worries. It will be wonderful that you can rejoice and be glad with God, and knowing you found a friend. We always think the worst, and that it's impossible for something good to come out of a bad situation. I heard a good man say one time, "when you are down to nothing God is up to something."

Matthew 19:26 states; With men this is impossible; but with God all things are possible.

People will tell you that you can't overcome your hurt, but if you put your trust in God you can do it. People will tell you I wouldn't forgive them for what they done to me, and they will always label them as being as Pedophiles even though they go to God and change their lives. It will be a sad thing if we die with unforgiving in our hearts. If we just read the Bible it has all of our answer to all of our questions.

Matthew 18:21-22 states, Then came Peter to him, and said, Lord, how oft shall my brother sin against me, and I forgive him? Till seven times?

22 Jesus saith unto him, I say not unto thee, Until seven times: but, Until seventy times seven.

Many times you have to forgive someone for doing you wrong, but if God said it, that makes it right. Jesus went to Calvary's cross for us, and yet he told his

Father, forgive them; for they know not what they do. (Luke 23:34),

Jesus got up with all power in his hand. So any little problem we have Jesus all ready paid the price for it. So lets give it to him and leave it with him, so he can fix it. Whenever we try to fix things ourselves it never come out right, because we don't have the power only God has that power. The power to loose you of your infirmities, and anything that's keeping you from glorifying Him.

If we stay around positive people that will also help us. We can make it through the storm with the help of others. Someone who is determine to go with us all the way without giving up. Also someone who have faith that God can healed you from any infirmity. In the Bible it tells us about a man borne of four was sick with palsy, he had the faith if he could just make it to Jesus, he would be healed, and his friends had that faith also. They didn't give up because they couldn't get through the door to see Jesus. They kept going until they figured out a way to get their friend healed from palsy. As a determine team they lifted their friend up, still lying in his bed onto the rooftop. They broke the roof and let down the bed as their friend still lye.

Mark 2:5 states; When Jesus saw their faith, he said unto the sick of the palsy, thy sins be forgiven thee.

Mark 2:11-12, I say unto thee, Arise, and take up thy bed, and go thy way unto thine house.

12 And immediately he arose, took up the bed, and went forth before them all; insomuch that they were all amazed, and glorified God, saying, we never we never saw it on this fashion.

I'm here to let you know that God is still in the healing business. God, he can deliver you out of any bad problems you think you can't get over. If he did back then he can do it now just try him.

Matthew 17:20 And Jesus said unto them, Because of your unbelief: for verily I say unto you. If ye have faith as a grain of mustard seed, ye shall say unto this mountain, Remove hence to yonder place; and it shall remove; and nothing shall be impossible unto you.

God gives us the power, and all we have to do is speak to that situation and it shall move. That's the kind of power we have to use to help ourselves. I would like for you to know Keenan spoke to the mountain one day. When he was fed up with the life he was living. Keenan went to AA meetings but he still went back to drinking. What is anonymous? Who are we hiding from? Everyone knows what you are, because they see what you are doing, because you don't hide when you are drinking your alcohol. He was also was a crack attic for twelve years, and he tried to stop on his own many of times. He would quit for awhile, then he would go back and meet the same people who he hung around, and he started back smoking again. This happen over and over again for twelve years. **How many of you know you got to change your life style in order to change your situation?** One day he decided to give it to God, and he left the state he was living in, and move to a different state. That's when we met, and he has been giving his situation it to God every since. Now Keenan is a Deacon at the church where we attend together. Don't tell me God want do it for you, I know what he can do, I tried him for myself and he is still making good things happen for me.

Parents listen to your children when they try and come to you with their problems. Please don't brush them off like you're not concern. Teach your children how to keep themselves. Watch their clothing, I know you are saying, "I wear what I want." A Pedophile also watches what you wear that's why you have to be aware of your surroundings. Pedophiles are watching your little girls and little boys. It's our job to protect them the best we know how. Even though I live in a small town it has happen here numerous of times. This is something we can't blot out of our minds, and people are becoming a victim every two minutes. Some times when our children try to come to us we think they are lying. Out of the mouth of babes they do tell the truth. Parents know where your children are at all times. Keep the communication line open, and make your children knowledgeable about life. Let them know they can't trust everyone, and not to let people lead them in dangerous places. Sit down and have family dinners at the table, and ask your children how their day was. Having family outings at least once a week is good for the whole family. Most of all attend church with your children. Every mother needs to gain her children's trust in order to talk to them about situation in their lives. If you spend a lot of time with your child you will know when they a being truthful. The majority of times when they tell something went wrong they are telling the truth. If you know without a doubt that your child is not a liar you can believe them if they tell you they were tampered with. Statistics shows five out of ten men that are living with a woman with children he is molesting them. It also shows that the natural father of the children is about four out of ten. Some men seek for women who have daughters just to violate them. There was a Mother of the church would always tell the young woman her husband died young. She also told them she wouldn't let another man be over her daughters. She explained to us her purpose was to not let her daughters be violated. After her husband died she didn't remarry or didn't have a boyfriend. She let us know that she had more respect for herself and her children. I encourage you to listen to the mothers of your church they will make you look at things differently. That mother talked with wisdom and knowledge. She didn't sugar coat things in order for you to be her friend. She loved making sure the young woman understand the correct way to do things. She taught and we listen to whatever she had to say about anything and everything. She was what you would call a season mother full of wisdom. I really and truly loved that mother from the bottom of my heart. She just didn't pray for her family she prayed for every family in the church. We need that kinds of mother in our church today in order to help us. That kind of church mother will also give you a good understanding about life, because they have been there and done that. That church mother would always say I don't want yawl out there looking for men. She said to make it right the man suppose to find the woman. We have the women of today that goes fishing for their man. The Internet is full of find your sweetheart sights. If you are a single mother why would you search the web for a man? I'm not saying all men are bad, but it's our job to protect our children. I want you to know there are over three hundred registered sex offenders just in my parish. Then we have those that haven't registered to keep it a secret. Those are the ones who we trust our kids with until the child tells. Then later on we find out on the evening news he's an unreported sex offender. Then you child becomes the next damaged man or woman. Pedophiles are everywhere and we don't know who they are, or their location. The people that own these types of web sites don't care if you make a love connection. All they want is that dollar ninety-nine a minute they are charging you, everything has a price ladies. How can you trust someone you have never met? They have some woman talk on the Net for only two weeks then get married. You can barely trust the ones you look at everyday we need to start thinking woman. Don't put yourself or your child out there to become the next damage woman or man. We as women need to know that the man for us will find us. So when your children come to you listen at their cry for help. Don't think the man in your life is so innocent you can't believe your children. You can stop your child from being another statistic gone wrong, and help keep them to have a stable mind. I know what you are saying, that's not going to happen to me. Well I didn't think it would happen to me either, but it did.

I (Lorner Jones) have a family member that is serving a twenty-five to life sentence right now for raping another family member. Can you tell me how sick is that? He said he didn't realize whom he was violating. My answer was "it didn't matter if she was or was not related to you she was a child." I didn't want to believe this certain relative of mine would do something this horrific but he did.

We need to be there for our children when they need us to be. Adults are suppose to be a good role model for their children, lets not set a bad example to ruin them. We can either help them or damage them which would you rather do? Be that someone who can be there in the time of need, and with an encouraging word. If your child ask for help that mean they need your help. Every since I was a little girl I would hear the grown ups say the children are our future. It's time we start making this saying come true. We need to start taking better care of our children, because they are not just our future they are now. At this very moment is the present, and anything beyond it is further, and that's the future, and that's now.

So let God be your guide in everything you do.

John15: 5 states, I am the vine, ye are the branches: He that abideth in me, and I in him, the same bringeth forth much fruit: for without me ye can do nothing.

Once we learn that we can't do anything without God the better we will be. This is a very important scripture that you can read to lift you up, and when things aren't going your way. *Psalm 27 The Lord is my light and my salvation; whom shall I fear? The Lord is the strength of my life; of whom shall I be afraid?*

2 When the wicked, even mine enemies and my foes, came upon me to eat up my flesh, they stumbled and fell.

3 Though an host should encamp against me, my heart shall not fear: though war should rise against me, in this will I be confident.

4 One thing have I desired of the Lord, that will I seek after; that I may dwell in the house of the Lord all the days of my life, to behold the beauty of the Lord, and to enquire in his temple. 5 For in the time of trouble he shall hide me in his pavilion: in the secret of his tabernacle shall he hide me; he shall set me upon a rock.

6 And now shall mine head be lifted up above mine enemies round about me: therefore will I offer in his tabernacle sacrifices of joy; I will sing, yea, I will sing praises unto the Lord.

I want you to know reading this scripture will get you through a lot of your difficult situations. I still say just give it to God and he will do the rest for you. Oh it don't matter what is or what looks like, ***look at it again***

Philippians 4: 13 said, I can do all things through Christ which strengtheneth me.

Meaning if this mean getting over rape, abuse, drug habits, sorrow, confused mind, jealousy, hatred, alcohol, unforgiving, lust, or any other demonic spirit that's holding me down I will do it. You are asking do what? I will submit myself to God. I can sit here and type a hundred pages or a thousand pages and they will all be the base on *God loosed me and I'm still glorifying him*.

If I had to preach that right now, I would tell you to look at your neighbor and say, **a brand new life.**

My autobiography

I Lorner Jeane Jones was born, and I grew up in ElDorado, Arkansas in a place called Memphis Heights with three of my sisters, and Grandparents. My mother also lived there, but on the other side of town with two of my other sisters, and two of my brothers. There are ten of her children still living, seven girls and three boys. I am the seventh child, and was born in the seven month, and seven is God's number. Growing up we wasn't allowed to go anywhere so we didn't know much about life, and it was a mystery to us. They taught us about school and work, and we had to be honor students, and we were. When it came to life situations we was very dumb. I thought I knew enough to run away from home, and that's what I done, and it was the biggest mistake of my life. I was badly misused by lots of people that I knew and I didn't know. Over the years I learned a lot about life and people. Some how I made through all the hurt, and the pain. Everything I went through, "I'm here to tell you it really made me stronger." I stayed on the streets awhile until I found out that I had to make a choice. I had to go live with my mother or go to a Juvenile home. I chose to go with my mother, and we moved to Zachary, La. Where I attended school, and also graduated from that school May 25, 1978. In Dec. of 1979 I moved to Sulphur, La., and I am still living there. I had three children, two boys, and one girl (one of my sons is deceased). I also have seven grandchildren five boys, and two girls. My father (Albert Jones) died May of 1980. Grandmother (Lillie Williams) died, Dec. of 1987, four days before Christmas. One of my brothers (Lawrence Elliott) was murdered in 1985. Mother (Margaret Washington) died Nov. of 1996; she was laid to rest four days before Thanksgiving. My oldest son (Kelvin Wilkerson) was murdered outside of his home in San Diego, Ca. Sept. 30, 2000. My grandfather (Booker T. Williams) died, in ElDorado, Ark. Dec. of 2000 he was laid to rest five day before Christmas. But through it all God brought me through. I can tell people after all I been through I still have joy. When my father, grandmother, and my brother died I was not save, and I didn't know how to handle it. When my mother, son, and grandfather died I was save, and with God it was much easier to bear. It makes a big difference when you are serving God, because your trials are easier to handle. I can say, "without God it would have been a disaster in the land." Over the years having God on my side everything got easier to handle. I am married to a wonder man now, and we are serving God together. We have two special friends Elder Derrick and Cassie Gallien. I have that friend whom we talk all the time Patricia Budwine. I have four Godchildren Kyresha Hardy, Derrick Gallien Jr., Jada Owens, and Angel Brown.

I really love my family and my husband's family especially my Mother-in- law, Father-in-law, sister-in-laws, and brother-in- laws. The reason I love them so much, because they treat me so special. I also work for a great co. I have been employed there over twenty years. I can truly say God has made a difference in my life.

My favorite scripture is **Psalm 34** here's just a few verses.

Psalm 34:1-8 I will bless the Lord at all times: his praise shall continually be in my mouth.

2 My soul shall make her boast in the Lord: the humble shall hear thereof, and be glad.

3 O magnify the Lord with me, and let us exalt his name together.

4 I sought the Lord, and he heard me, and delivered me from all my fears.

5 They looked unto him, and were lightened: and their faces were not ashamed.

6 This poor man cried, and the Lord heard him, and saved him out of all his troubles.

7 The angel of the Lord encampeth round about them that fear him, and delivereth them.

8 O taste and see that the Lord is good: blessed is the man that trusteth in him.

The scriptures were taken out of the King James Bible version

Luke 13:10-13
James 4:7
James 1:14-15
John 8:36
Romans 7:18
1ˢᵗ John 1:9
Romans 8: 5
John 8:32
Ecclesiastes 12: 14
Matthew 6:14-15
1ˢᵗ Corinthians 10:13
Proverbs 3:5-6
Psalms 121:1-2
Matthew 19:26
2ⁿᵈ Corinthians 12:9
Matthew 18:21-22
Matthew 11:28-30
Luke 23:34
Hebrews 11:6
Mark 2:5
Revelation 3:20-21

Mark 2: 11-12
Galatians 6:7-9
Matthew 17:20
Matthew 24:35
John 15:5
2ⁿᵈ Corinthians 5:17
Psalm 27:1-6
Philippians 4:13
Hebrews 10:30
Mark 5:1-9
Romans 12:19
1ˢᵗ Peter 5:8
Matthew 9:20-21
Proverbs 18:22
Matthew 26:39
Matthew 17:14-20
Leviticus 20:13
Revelations 12:11

A special thanks goes to:

Keenan Wynn Sallier Sr.

Towashai' Jones

Reginald K. Jones

Rameka Cuba- Jones

LeAndrus Bradley

Patricia Budwine

Lorraine Moore

Lyndrea Hawkins

Addie Hawthrone

Frank Sallier

Joyce Sallier

Steve Clark

Toma M. Sallier

Harold Sallier Jr.

Chad K. Sallier

Shamekka Thomas

Tara D. Owens

James Owens Sr.

Ebony E. Sallier

Porsha A. Celestine

Keenan W. Sallier Jr.

Kimberly Angelle

Supt. Rogers Cain

Thelma M. Cain

Elder Charles E. Porter Sr.

Carol L. Porter

Rhonda Eglin- Jourdan

Jimmie Lee Williams

John Charles Hall

Charlsie Ann Smith

Cecilia Nation

Booker T. Washington

Tyra Evans

Velma Parker

Endorlurree Nation

Zefforia Nation

Bobby Nation

And to all other family
and friends

I also have some special co- workers

Patricia Budwine
Laura Roberts
Joann Williams
Charlotte Freeman
Beverly Rainwater
Charlita Harrison
Lorraine Moore
Tameka Mitchell
Rosie Wilson

I was inspired to write this inspirational story Damaged Women, because I see many women, men, and children that are afraid. I saw myself in them, and I know what they are going through. I have been through a lot of damaging situation to last a lifetime.

Until I got enough courage to seek help for myself, I was just like everyone else lost in the house. Some people get help others don't know how, and this is where I come in to help them. Just letting them know what I have been through, and how God delivered me. I hope this will help women in their time of needing someone to be there for them. It's not easy to admit that you need help, but once you do, everything begins to go in the right direction for you. I know some situations need more care than others need.

Philippians 4:13 states; I can do all things through Christ which strengthened me.

God gave me the strength to overcome my past, and he can help you overcome yours also. I know what I can do with God's help, and I know he will lead me to help others. I don't mind telling my testimony to whoever wants to listen. We are not in this world alone; we still have people that care. Being able to be someone's friend in the time in his or her time of trouble can be a great thing. Especially if you been through a similar situation, and have been delivered. I'm writing to let everyone know that there is still hope. There is a bright light at the end of all tunnels. I'm here to let you know God will make away out of no way. *"I still say no matter how it looked the first time you looked at it, look at it again."*

Luke 13:10-13 talks about how Jesus healed a woman with an eight-teen year infirmity and when he did she glorified Him. If I had to preach that right now, "I would say look at your neighbor and say **a brand new life.**

www.ingramcontent.com/pod-product-compliance
Lightning Source LLC
Chambersburg PA
CBHW031302280526
45784CB00004B/1962